Paper Sculpture

The author at work on paper sculpture inspired by the ballet *Les Sylphides*

PAPER SCULPTURE

By

ARTHUR SADLER, F.R.S.A.

LONDON

BLANDFORD PRESS

First published 1946
Second Edition 1951
Third Edition 1954
Fourth Edition 1958

*Printed in Great Britain by Tonbridge Printers Ltd., Tonbridge, Kent,
and published by Blandford Press Ltd.,
16 West Central Street, London, W.C.1*

Foreword

I was first impressed with Paper Sculpture as a form of decoration from examples seen at various exhibitions on the Continent, and as a result of its fascinating appearance experimented in the production of small pieces and designs as a hobby.

Patience and experience gained from constant mistakes resulted in creations which were employed to good effect in window displays, and requests were made for me to teach the craft to others. It is with that object in view that this book has been written.

Whilst great pleasure can be derived from paper sculpture as an artistic hobby, its practical applications for all engaged in display and publicity work are as interesting as they are varied. Expense does not enter into the question since the material required can be obtained cheaply, and variation in design is dependent wholly on the ingenuity of the creator.

Do not imagine that the shop window or interior is the only place in which paper sculpture can be used to obtain artistic effects. Ample opportunities are available for its employment as a form of decoration in public buildings, exhibitions, schools, cinema foyers, advertisement layouts and for photography.

The reader will realise that it is often far easier to demonstrate the creation of a given piece of work than it is to describe the various stages in words; forbearance is therefore sought if the seemingly simplest details have been over emphasised in an effort to provide clarity and understanding of the technique required for building different models.

In addition to my own creations, examples of the work of some of the most talented artists in paper sculpture are illustrated to show the variety of applications to which the craft can be applied, and it is my sincere hope that commercial users, teachers and students will derive stimulus and knowledge from the information provided.

ARTHUR SADLER

Contents

Contents *(cont.)*

Contents *(cont.)*

"Those Were the Days," by the author

A study from the ballet *Les Sylphides* in paper sculpture by the author

Paper Sculpture

Occasionally in the history of the graphic arts, artistic experiment evolves a really new technique. In the course of time this may develop into a new art form. From the centuries old methods of peasant paper craft, Paper Sculpture as we see it today has followed that course. This firmly established and expressive medium is a commercial art form in its own right. In fact, based as it is on the building up of relief from sheet materials, it differs greatly in primary concept and manipulative technique from all familiar media.

Modelling in paper is as old as the invention of paper itself which, Chinese tradition says, was invented in A.D. 105.

But it is in Poland where the beginnings of the craft must be sought in the paper flowers which were fashioned to adorn the shrines in village homes. Christmas paper decorations were also made and these peasant patterns became a real inspiration for the professional artist. Here started ideas for the artistic use of paper in three dimensions—the birth of PAPER SCULPTURE. Later composition in paper was introduced into the syllabus of Polish art schools. Annual balls at the Academy of Art in Warsaw saw the appearance of large decorative panels, grotesque human figures, pseudo architectural detail and bas-reliefs, all executed in paper by some of Poland's artists who were also famous for their work in other spheres.

It was a natural sequence that some of this work found its way into window displays and advertising. The shortage of conventional materials in Central Europe during the First World War prompted ingenious artists of that region to turn to this form of peasant art. In fact, however, such a title was no longer deserved, so sophisticated had some of the designs become interpreting the modern idiom prevalent in Europe in 1918. Sculptural fully rounded figures of paper were built, solidity being achieved through the bending and folding of the material which had been characteristic of the prototypes.

When exhibitions started again on the Continent buyers of commercial art and advertising, always eager for a new and striking approach, commissioned some of these artists to make attractions in paper sculpture. They were an instant success. It was not until Polish artists commercialised its application at Continental exhibitions that English and American artists commenced sporadic efforts with the craft. World War II came and many of Poland's artists took up residence in England and America and, as had been the case in 1918, the shortage of decorative materials once again made numerous artists turn to paper sculpture as a medium for artistic expression.

The work of these Polish artists was regarded as a European importation and, therefore, as something of especial virtue. English and American artists and students whose imagination was fired by its scope developed the ability to produce work in an original style and teachers added it to their curricula.

The further development of Paper Sculpture has resulted from the activities of many artists and, naturally, educationalists, advertisers and display men soon realised its possibilities and in these fields it is now being used the world over.

Principles of Paper Sculpture

Paper sculpture is evolved from sheets of paper so rolled, bent, scored, cut and folded that it makes a desired form. A sheet of paper is flat and two dimensional. Paper sculpture begins when the flat sheet of paper is curved or bent to produce more than a single plane. Fold a piece of paper once and immediately you have two surfaces, one going away from you in space and one coming toward you. By curving and folding a third dimension is created.

Paper can be rolled into a tube and will support itself on end. If the paper is stout enough it will withstand a weight many times its own. As paper is bent it gains strength and its roundness gives an appearance of bulk and solidity.

Paper sculpture takes advantage of the fact that bent paper is stronger than the same material in a flat sheet, a mere shell giving the illusion of volume. The sculptor must manipulate his material into an appearance of the form desired and portray simplified and flattened planes into a "solid" effect.

Paper itself limits and restricts to a natural simplicity of design. The most important thing to remember is that paper has a limited range of form and it is only the *effect* of the characteristic contours of the subject being portrayed which can be represented.

Varieties of Paper

Of all the simple materials made by man, paper is the most easily workable, is universally available, and inexpensive. Made in great variety, it has a wide range in weight—from tissue to cardboard. The weight suitable for paper sculpture depends, of course, upon the size of the model to be made. Small pieces can be made of lightweight paper; large must be made of a heavier type. Nothing lighter than cartridge paper should be used. Most of the author's work has been constructed from Whatman drawing paper in medium weight, rough or smooth surface, depending upon the effect desired. For coloured work, this material can easily be sprayed with a gun or tinted by hand.

Ready-coloured papers—such as poster paper—are not suitable for paper sculpture unless mounted on a stouter sheet. Even so, there is the risk that the scoring will expose the under sheet.

This same objection applies to many papers which have a surface colour only—such as an overlay of foil or thin coloured paper. They are not suitable for scoring, since the cracked surface exposes the undercolour. Paper coloured throughout in manufacture is, of course, highly suitable; so too is wood-veneer paper which is not mounted on a white sheet.

Another important item to know is the sizes of paper available, which govern, of course, the size of sculptures made in one piece. Ingenuity in placing one piece over another will, however, overcome this difficulty to a considerable extent.

Coloured papers which carry a definite pattern or design must be handled with discretion, since they call attention to themselves, upset sculptural conventions, and obscure form.

Despite the varieties of paper at his disposal, the paper sculptor will settle down to work with the few specific types that he likes best. Some use nothing but white paper in varying weights, finding that ingenuity of handling counts for more than a show of resources.

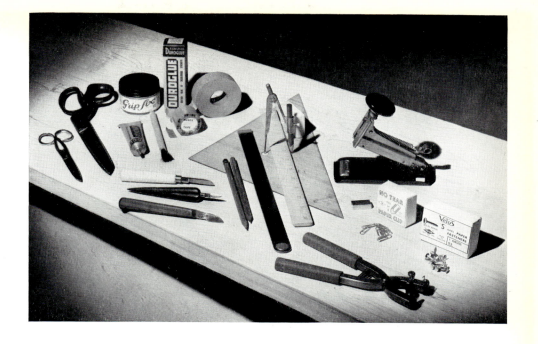

Tools and Materials

Basic tools required for paper sculpture are so simple that many will be found in the majority of homes:

PAPER   For classroom and experimental purposes ordinary drawing paper may be used. For more advanced work, use cartridge paper and Whatman drawing paper in rough and smooth texture according to the type of work required.

SCISSORS   to use only when more convenient than a knife for cutting out the shapes.

KNIVES   can be of any type with a short sharp blade.

GLUES   Quick-drying adhesives are best. Duroglue for heavy paper. Gripfix for lighter work, are recommended.

STAPLER   of the office type illustrated, to join paper together or to fasten paper to a background.

PINS, PAPER PINS, PAPER FASTENERS.

GUMMED TAPE   to use on the back of bent surfaces. This gives extra strength.

DRAWING INSTRUMENTS: set-square, compasses, wooden ruler, metal ruler, pencils.

PAPER PUNCH: the type used for leather work is useful, but not essential.

Cutting Paper and Cardboard

Knives of any description can be used for cutting. A pad of old cardboard or paper between the bench and the object being cut not only protects the bench top, but gives the work a bed that keeps it from slipping. The pad will, of course, need renewing from time to time when it becomes cut to such an extent that it does not provide a smooth surface.

To cut a straight line, use a metal rule or guide which should be held firmly against the paper with the left hand. The right hand holding the knife should be more relaxed than the left, since the blade will require very little pressure to cut through the paper. Students of paper sculpture will be well advised to have pencil lines to follow for both cutting and scoring: eye and hand co-ordinate in following a pencilled line.

All shapes should be cut out with a knife rather than scissors—a knife gives a cleaner cut. The worker will eventually find his favourite cutting tool, which may be a razor blade, a knife or a stencil knife. The latter is a very useful implement for young students, and is safe to handle.

Decorative effects can be obtained by using pinking shears to cut the paper, or hole punchers as used for leather work. These latter are useful not only for lace effects in paper, but the circles they cut can be used for decorative effects, as may be seen in some of the illustrations in this book.

To cut cardboard with a knife, do not try to press hard and cut in one stroke. Cut with several even strokes, following the same line carefully, until the cardboard is separated from end to end. The start and end always require an extra stroke or so, depending upon whether you are an enthusiastic starter or finisher! Sharp tools are essential; see that the knife is sharpened frequently on a whetstone with oil, paying attention to the point as well as to the blade edge.

Scoring Paper and Cardboard

Scoring is one of the most used methods in folding paper and card. The process means that the paper surface is cut half-way through so that the paper will bend away from the cut surface.

To score, bear very lightly on the knife blade. The exact amount of pressure required should be determined by trial cuts on scraps of paper or card. The correct amount of pressure is important. If the scoring is made too deeply, the paper will break away when folded. In scoring a straight line, a metal ruler should be used as a guide.

Curling
Paper

Paper may be curled for decorative purposes by passing it between the thumb and a scissor blade as shown above. Take a strip of paper, hold with one hand and place the paper over the scissor blade, with the thumb on top. Draw the thumb and scissor blade down the paper and a curl will be effected. This curling is applied to such things as hair styles on paper figures, flower petals, etc. This method also will make paper pliable.

Basic Shaping

Paper can be shaped in two basic ways to give an effect of roundness and solidity—either by bending or folding. If bent it should be rolled the way of the grain of the paper. Paper bends easily but always in one direction and in a more or less geometrical form. For full roundness it can be bent into tubes and cones, or for low relief effects bent only part of the way round forming an arc. The cylinder in all variations is the foundation of paper sculpture in the round.

When paper is folded to give a sharp transition from one plane to another an angular break made by scoring is used. If a piece of paper is bent along a straight line note that one side catches the light. Paper folded into a series of reverse folds will break up a flat surface into a pattern of light and shade. Variations of bending are corrugating and curling.

All these methods are demonstrated and one can soon learn how to manipulate paper and create designs that have as much art quality as those done in other media.

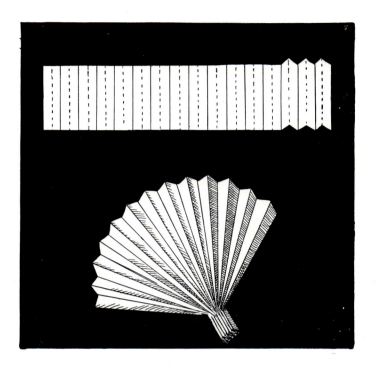

A Fan

Take a piece of drawing paper approximately 16 inches long and 10 inches wide. With a pencil, mark off in ½-inch spaces on both sides of the paper.

With a scoring knife and metal ruler, score every other line on one side of the paper only. (See black line in sketch.) Turn the paper over and score the lines which are *not* scored on the other side.

Holding the paper in both hands, fold it back and forth, thus producing a pleated strip. Pinch one end and fan out the other.

There may appear to be little in this simple exercise, but if it has taught you the meaning of scoring, folding and pleating, then three very important methods employed in paper sculpture will have been mastered.

The fold is one of the commonest devices used in the craft; the sharp turn from one plane to another suggest depth and also catches the light. Notice, too, that pleating stiffens paper, as does bending into a tube.

A Star

On a piece of drawing paper, draw a five-pointed star. With a scoring knife, score light lines from each point to their common meeting place at centre (Fig. 1).

Cut the star round the outline with the knife.

Turn the star over, and score lines from the centre to the crotches (Fig. 2). Using both hands to fold, ridge the long scores up, and fold the short scores down. Use the knife blade to obtain sharp folds at the centre.

Thus is a five-pointed star produced—something distinctive and pleasing, far superior to the plain cut-out, and the lesson has been learnt that paper can be folded by the way it is scored. For instance, scored on one side it could be folded down; on the reverse side it could be folded up.

Cone

Formation

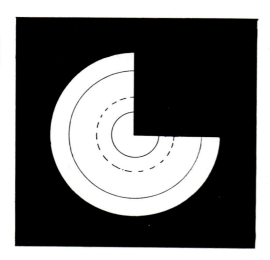

To make a cone, all that is required is a circle with a segment removed and the edges joined together.

Now try the diagram shown. Draw a circle and cut it out. On this circle draw three inner circles, two on one side (black lines on diagram) and one on the reverse side (dotted line). Score these circles and cut out a quarter-segment of the circle. Bend the scoring on both sides, mould into a cone and secure. Now you will have the form shown in the photograph standing at the back, also laid flat on the extreme left.

The other forms shown are a plain cone and a cone with one circle scored into it. You can see that variations can be made by sculpturing a plain surface in this way.

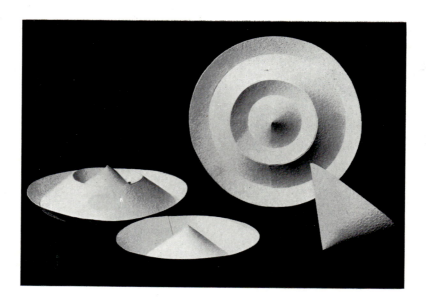

Draw pattern as below. Cut out as shown and on one side draw a circle as indicated by the black line.

Turn the pattern over and draw a circle slightly larger than the first (dotted line). Score round both circles (one on each side) and cut through from the outside to the centre of the flower. Pull "A" over "B", completely covering the whole petal, and stick down.

The centre scoring will now be in relief with a deep cone in the centre (see illustration). This is based on the example on previous page.

Small flowers are made in the same manner, with the exception that they have only one circle scored in the centre. Leaves for the setting do not require explanation.

The flowers may be arranged flat as shown on page 24, or they may be wired through the centre and arranged in groups, stamens hiding the wiring.

Stylised Flowers

Decorative designs suitable for garlands or for panel and border decorations,
by the author

Decorative Swags

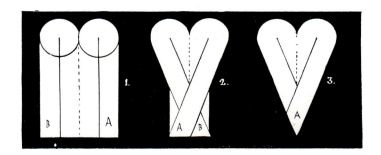

The decorative swag shown on the opposite page can be used for many purposes, and looks particularly attractive in white on wedgwood blue, or in gold on red.

Cut the shapes to the pattern as seen at the top of this page, in three sizes, and cut down the long black lines to the centre of the circles. (The circles have been left as a guide in drawing the pattern.)

Score down the dotted line, and fold. Cross the pieces "A" and "B", pulling the end circle pieces round at the same time; stick together at their crossing place and cut off surplus paper.

Note that these shapes are based upon the cone formation—the circular ends spliced to form the cones.

The finished pieces can be assembled to form the swag shown on opposite page, or as a frame (page 51).

The laurel swag is dealt with next. Cut laurel leaf shapes, score, fold and assemble them in threes as illustrated, and overlap in groups. Two swags would make a "wreath of honour," a decoration often required in display and advertising presentations.

Stylised Flowers

Flower Study, "Daffodils," by the author

Draw and cut out as diagram. Score dotted lines on one side and the black lines on the reverse side. Cut a circle out of the centre and bend the scoring on both sides. This will give an attractive shape. (See photograph below.)

To make a daffodil: First make a cone and place through the hole in the centre of the flower shape and fix by placing a circle of gum tape over the cone where it protrudes at the back of the flower. Place a wire through the centre of the cone for a stem, and finish by wrapping the wire with thin paper.

Flower variations shown are two of the flower shapes placed over each other at an angle with a piece of rolled paper for the centre (*bottom right*).

The flower shape in reverse, with a thin, frilled paper centre (*top right*).

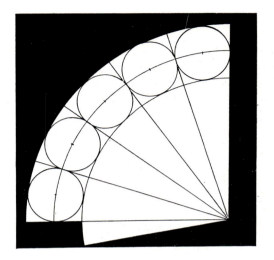 

To draw the pattern for the stylised lilies, draw a circle 12 inches in diameter. Inside this draw another circle 10 inches diameter and again another circle 9 inches diameter. Draw five circles $1\frac{1}{2}$ inches diameter, using the $10\frac{1}{2}$ inch circumference as centres (see sketch). Draw lines to the centre from where these five smaller circles touch. Next add a small section as shown on the drawing. This is to stick the cone of the lily together.

Cut the shape out and also cut between the petals down to the inner circle. Rub out all pencil marks. Curl the petals with the scissor blades. Make into a cone and secure by glueing the small section. The stamens are strips of paper bent at the ends. For the stem, place a stout wire through the centre of the lily and wrap with thin paper, inserting leaves at intervals.

Flower Study by the author

Flower Study by Angus Basil, F.I.B.P.

Sculptured Frame

Trace and cut out in stiff drawing paper four of the shapes from pattern. Score them and fold to shape. Reverse your pattern and make another four shapes. They are next arranged on a flat cardboard frame, $15\frac{1}{2} \times 12 \times 2$ inches. They can be pinned or fixed with seccotine where they touch the frame. The flowers in the frame are shown on page 32.

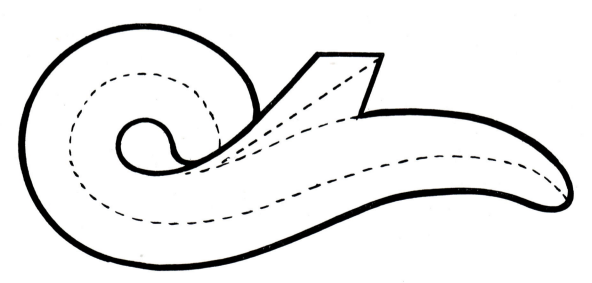

Trace the pattern on to draw-ing paper, cut out and curl the petals, fold into a cone and stick. When dry, pinch each petal where shown by dotted line. Wire in the usual way. The leaves need no explanation.

Flowers

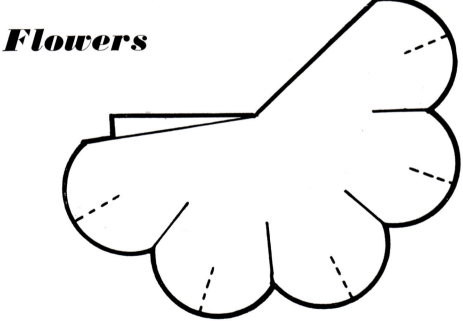

Curves

To become acquainted with curves, first draw an "S" formation and cut out. Score with a knife down the centre, following the shape, and mould by bending the scoring to the "S" shape. It will be seen how this multi-scoring and moulding strengthens the paper and how these curved pieces can be manipulated into beautiful forms.

Making
Baroque
Shapes

Twelve feet in length, this balcony was constructed from baroque-effect scrolls by the author. Mounted against a sky-blue background, it provides an excellent setting for fashion merchandise, or a background for photographic purposes

Most people are fascinated by the baroque-effect scrolls in paper sculpture, which look very difficult to produce but are, in fact, quite simple with a little practice.

First, draw the shapes as shown in the sketch on a stout cartridge paper. Cut them out, following the thick black lines, and follow this line round the inner scrolls. After cutting out, draw with a pencil the dotted lines as shown in the sketch. The next stage is to score these dotted lines with the knife.

With both hands, fold up the scores in ridges, moulding to the shape of the scroll as you progress.

These scrolls are very useful for decorating panels or for making frames; the latter are prepared by arranging the shapes in the baroque method upon a flat white frame.

This design is a sample arrangement of the shapes described.

A Baroque Frame

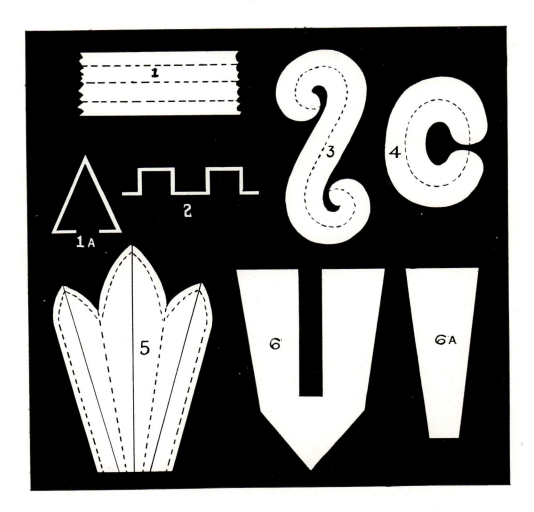

To make the frame shown opposite, a wallboard frame for a foundation is required. This should be covered with white paper.

The straight moulding for the frame (Fig. 1) is made from paper strips scored and made into a triangular shape (1A).

The crenelated moulding also is made from paper strips, scored and made up as in Fig. 2.

The curved shapes (Figs. 3 and 4) are scored and made up. Shape 4 is bent round and fastened underneath with a paper clip. Pattern 5 is cut out, scored and made up. Patterns 6 and 6A are cut out and curled.

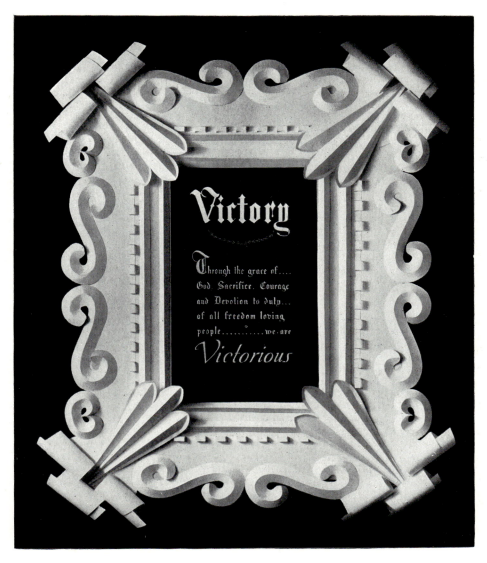

Victory

Through the grace of....
God. Sacrifice. Courage
and Devotion to Duty...
of all freedom loving
people............we are
Victorious

By the author

To assemble the shapes on the frame, begin by glueing the straight and crenelated moulding. Follow with the curves, placing them over the edge of the straight frame. Then scroll 6A and 6, followed by shape 5 which completes the corner.

White Framed Mirror
with Candle Holders

By the author

This frame in all-white sculpture would be an ideal set-piece for a display of beauty products, or in a fashion presentation. It is quite simple to make.

First requirement is a stout foundation cut slightly *under* actual size of the frame, covered with metallic or mirror paper.

The frame is cut from stout white paper; score round the outside and fold as shown and fix to the foundation.

The moulding round the mirror is cut out, scored and folded, and at the same time moulded round to fit the opening. Note that the moulding must be cut *across*, and also overlaps. Apply paste to the overlaps, and fasten to frame.

The scrolls are next to receive attention. Score, fold, and fix them to frame. Cut, score, and fold the carved-effect roses; pull "A" to "B" and stick. Cut and fold the leaves, and assemble the top group to the frame.

Make a cardboard box with two holes as illustrated, and fasten to frame with paper pins.

The two candles are paper tubes with cut-out flames, and are inserted in the holes provided in the box.

Cover the box with a group of roses, and the mirror is completed.

This idea could, of course, be used to frame other sculptured set-pieces by removing the box and candles.

39

Construction

Anyone with a faculty for making things can soon develop the knack of assembling paper sculpture. Although each piece made will present its own construction problems the methods explained here will be of assistance until the sculptor develops new ones by experimenting with paper.

Low relief paper sculptures are usually supported on a cardboard or other heavy foundation, cut to the outline of the design. Layers of paper are then curved over this foundation and secured behind it with paper tabs. Pieces to stand by themselves, unless they have a tube of cone base such as a figure of a lady in a crinoline, will need a cardboard strut for support. In some cases this can be a part of the sculpture such as the off-side legs of an animal. Large subjects for which a cardboard base will not give sufficient support need a wooden construction. In the construction of large pieces of sculpture, paper tabs will not be strong enough to hold the paper to the foundation. Wire staples can be used for this purpose. To place these anywhere but near the edge, a staple gun of the type used by displaymen is essential, or, failing this, a desk stapler removed from its base. Failing either form of stapler, tacks can be used. The heads of staples or tacks must not show on the surface of the finished work. The top layer of paper must therefore be so designed as to hide traces of construction. This top layer can be attached with gum tape concealed beneath the edges. Another method is to cut two slits in each piece of paper and inset a strip of paper through these, then bending the ends back and securing with gum tape. This holds the two pieces together neatly. To keep one layer of paper above another so that it casts the shadows required to suggest solidity, pieces of paper or card tabbed at both ends can be used to keep the assemblies apart.

Large pieces of sculpture may have to be made in sections to allow for easier handling. In this connection cardboard hooks can be used in the construction. These fit into slots to hold the units of construction together. Much will be learned by trial and error. The examples given in this book should be practised first to gain the knowledge required to make ones own designs.

Toy soldier demonstrates how low-relief sculptured figures are constructed and how the pieces are tabbed to a card foundation.

Low-Relief Sculpture

Low-relief sculpture is like translating a drawing into paper relief; the foundation follows the simplified outline of the drawing. The paper overlays are sufficiently wide to allow for belling out and turning under, giving a solid effect.

Decorative details are built on to the main pieces of paper, just as finishing touches are worked into the sketched masses of a drawing. The scored lines control the bends, and folds are placed where an artist would indicate the crossing of planes or their recession.

The sketch shows a tree in low relief with the layers of paper held apart by tabbed paper and also hooks of cardboard to hold the units of construction together.

Full-Relief Sculpture

Small figures in full relief sculpture to stand by themselves are quite easy to construct on the cone and tube principle. Larger pieces to be seen from all sides require experience to produce good results.

For these figures sheets of paper are wrapped around a wooden support, forming them into cylinders and cones. The larger masses are modified by attaching transitional pieces between them and finally the small details are placed over all. The effect is like low relief sculpture but carried around on all sides.

Until the technique is acquired for making large pieces, it would be advisable to make a small model first, as it will be found easier to handle and fold small pieces of paper. The small model can then be taken apart, and the pieces spread out flat and used as patterns to enlarge to the required size.

Making a Chessman

On the opposite page is a photograph of a chessman which was executed in low-relief sculpture and was constructed to stand by itself. Let us attempt to reconstruct this figure.

First, the pattern marked (1) in the sketch should be cut out of cardboard to the size required; the other pieces are paper.

Next, cut out the mane pattern; (2) curl it backwards with scissor blades, and fasten it to the back of the base. Fold the scoring (3) up and the tabs back, and fasten them behind the base with gum. Fold and attach the ear (4), score and fold the eye (5), and attach tabs to the base.

Fold in the nostril (6) and attach to (5). Fold the scoring at (7) (8) and (9), and attach ornamental leaves. Place (11) in position, bowing it out as you do so, and finish with (10) at the top and (12) at the bottom.

Because of the width of the base, this figure will stand upright without additional support.

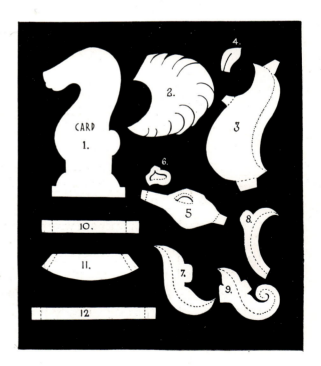

Low-relief figure of a white knight from a chess set, by the author

Making a Rooster

This model was executed in red and white paper. First, prepare a rough sketch of the bird, indicating where the rows of feathers are to be shown in relief, as in Fig. 1. From this pattern, trace to a sheet of cardboard the outline of the head, body and legs; this is the foundation. Now to make the paper sculpture covering.

Wing, Body and Tail Feathers

For the body and neck feathers, take a strip of drawing paper 3 inches wide, and cut into $\frac{1}{2}$-inch scallops.

With the scoring knife, score through the centre of each scallop and down each side as in Fig. 2. Wing feathers and short tail feathers are scored in the same manner, after having been cut to shape. These, you will notice, are cut pointed and not scalloped, from a wider strip of paper. The correct shape can be seen by referring to Fig. 3.

Next to be dealt with are the long tail feathers, which are cut separately as in Fig. 2. After cutting to shape, they are scored down the centre, the scoring following the shape of the feather.

Comb, Head and Wattles

Cut the comb and wattles to shape in paper, paint them in scarlet colour, and add the eye in black. The next step is to cut out a complete head, and on this mount comb and wattles. It should be noted that these portions are left flat, and are not creased in any way. A close-up view of the shapes can be seen displayed on a board in Fig. 3.

44

Folding and Pleating

The body feathers, wing feathers and short tail feathers are pleated as in making a paper fan (Fig. 3).

The long tail feathers are folded by scoring and moulding to shape; the creases following the contours of the feather (Fig. 3).

Assembling Complete Bird

Cut out the bird foundation, on which the sculptured patterns are to be assembled, and start with the neck feathers.

Place one row round the neck of the foundation, just under the position for the head feathers, curving them to your pattern in a rounded effect like opening a fan, and fasten behind the foundation. Underneath the first row, place other rows of feathers until completed.

Fix the complete head in position, overlapping the first row of neck feathers, thus giving a dimensional effect.

Next to be dealt with are the short tail feathers, the remaining body feathers, and the wing. For the legs, the cardboard of the foundation may be employed by cutting slenderly and sliding over tubes of paper to give full, round legs. The addition of spurs and claws completes the rooster.

A Cherub or Cupid

To make this cherub, a cardboard foundation is required (Fig. 1). Shapes are cut out, scored and folded where shown (Fig. 2) and are attached to the foundation by fixing with tabs.

Composition of the head is the same as given on page 67, where instructions will also be found for making features and curls for the cherub's hair.

Details of the wing construction will be found on page 44.

Head and wings are assembled to the body, and fixed to foundation.

Score and fold sash, bow and arrow, and fix in position.

The cherub illustrated was made in all-white paper; it would be still more striking in silver metallic paper.

This little fellow could be used for many decorative purposes, and would be especially suitable for a window display on St. Valentine's Day.

Minus the bow and arrow, it could be used to hold a garland of flowers, or to hold back draped curtains.

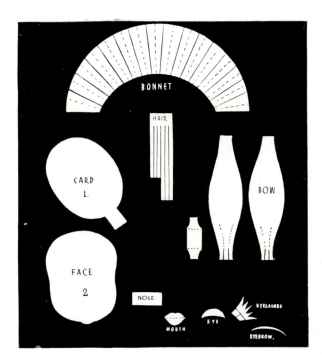

Cut a cardboard foundation (Fig. 1), then the face (Fig. 2).

Cut the mouth, score and fix to face. Mount eyelashes behind the eyes, and fix in position, and also the eyebrows.

Roll the nose piece and fix; fasten the face to the foundation and bow out the cheeks at the same time.

Curl the hair and fix in position.

Score and fold the bonnet, and fix behind the head fan-fashion.

Cut and score the bow ends, making two bow loops; finish by scoring the bow centre and cover the loops. Attach to the head beneath the chin, and the figure is completed.

The amusing baby's head would be especially attractive in a baby linen display.

Coloured papers should be used; pale blue or pink for the bonnet and bow, pale pink for the face, yellow for the hair, eyebrows and eyelashes, blue for the eyes; and the mouth should be shaped as a cupid's bow in bright red.

Constructed on the same principles as the baby's head, the girls' or boy's heads are suitable for displays of schoolwear, or to decorate a juvenile department; and Minnie Mouse would find favour with children as a decoration.

Amusing Heads

Sculptured Panel—Autumn

Here is an attractive head, for which a panel of wallboard or other stout material will be required for mounting figure and frame.

Cover the panel with wood-design paper and place a darker strip of paper round the edge as a border, making allowance for the frame. To this panel the head is fixed as it is made.

For the face, use a piece of wood-design paper (see sketch); cut an eye and two slots for the nose tabs, and a slit for the mouth. Bend this mask into an arc, and fasten with a paper clip.

Cut a piece of paper for the neck; crease where shown, bend round, and fasten with a clip. Insert neck in the headpiece and clip together.

Now for the forehead and nose. Score and fold as illustrated, fix the nose tabs into the slots cut in the face, bend the forehead round and fasten at the back of the head.

Fix the head and neck to the panel, bearing in mind that only half a head is being seen.

For the hair (Figs. 1, 2 and 3) cut, score, fold, and attach to head. (See photograph of finished design for positioning.) Add scarf and mouth, and one or two leaves cut and scored on the same principle.

The frame design, having the effect of a carving, is made from the same pattern as the decorative swag on page 25.

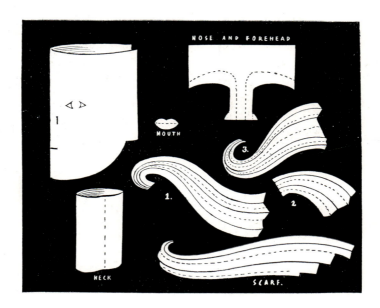

This head was made in wood-veneer paper, and has the effect of a wood carving. Paper was light oak with dark oak border, thus adding to the autumnal atmosphere. In addition to its uses for display purposes, this decorative panel would be ideal for the home.

Miss Amanda Rabbit

This sculpture should be made in coloured papers of a very heavy type, and requires a cardboard foundation. (See pattern.)

The body is cut out to pattern in pink paper, fastened to the foundation, and bowed out for the stomach.

The bonnet should be in pale blue paper, and is cut as indicated by the thick black line and trimmed with lace paper from a doily.

Pull part "A" over "B" and stick together. Fix the bonnet to the neck of the rabbit. Cut out the face shape and paint in the features; the cheek jowl should be cut round to the eye from the nose. Curving slightly, pull the cheek in slightly beneath the nose, and fasten with gummed tape at the rear. Pull the cheek to the right under the jowl and fix; this will impart a rounded face. Fix the face inside the bonnet with the cut-out mouth below the cheeks. Score the ears, fold, and fix behind the bonnet. Place paws and tail in the positions as shown in the photograph, and secure. Trim the bonnet with flowers in bright colours and add bonnet strings.

Stand Miss Rabbit in a hat box trimmed with flowers and lined with yellow tissue paper; trim the lid with sculptured flowers and bow, and the presentation is complete.

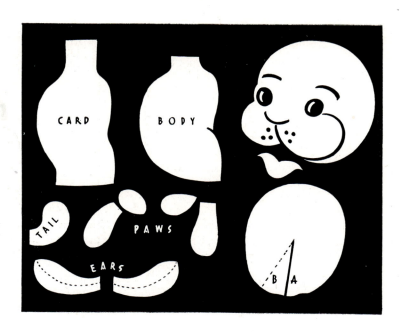

This delightful rabbit in her Easter bonnet would be ideal for a children's wear or millinery display. The example shown was in gay Easter colourings.

Decorative Fish Panel

To make this fish, cut out a foundation of cardboard to outline the head, body and tail.

Cut out the tail (1), score, fold, and attach to the foundation, fastening with the tabs behind.

On the body pattern (2) are some wavy black lines, which indicate slots to accommodate the fins, and should be cut through with a knife. Cut out patterns in black paper for the fins (3); score, fold, and insert in the slots of the body, fastening behind with gummed tape. The body should be fastened to the foundation and bowed out at the same time. (It will, of course, have been cut larger than the foundation to allow for bowing, as previously instructed.) Attach by tabs behind the foundation.

Score, fold and attach the fins behind the foundation (4), and lastly the head (5). Score and crease where shown; score and attach eyepieces and mouth (6).

Attach the head to the body, and the fish is complete.

Note should be taken of the method employed for inserting the fins into the body by slots. This method is also useful for inserting wings into the body of a bird.

The example shown was made in black and white paper, but
would look equally effective in coloured paper.

There is ample opportunity for colour treatment in undersea
scenes—starfish, lobsters, corals, etc.

Scottish Lion

Here is a simple piece of sculpture which can be used for a panel or background, and which does not require a foundation.

The lion is cut out of paper (Fig. 1) and scored and folded where indicated by the dotted lines. Next, the back leg (Fig. 2) is scored and folded, and placed behind the body and fixed with gummed tape, followed by the tail overlay (Fig. 3). Score and fold the overlay for the head (Fig. 4); score the tongue and fix to head (Fig. 5).

Before placing the head overlay in position on the main structure, fix a bridge—or tabbed piece of paper—to hold the overlay slightly apart from the body. This will cast a shadow and suggest greater depth—see photograph for effect.

This lion would be ideal for a decoration when featuring merchandise from Scotland. In the example shown, the background was composed of Scottish tweed.

Animal Figures

Here is a sketch showing the making of a paper lamb. As will be seen, construction is composed of tubes with the exception of the face and ears.

The figure is covered with curled paper made by slashing into strips and then curled.

Also sketched is a dog made on the tube and cone principle with details added.

This simple sketch shows the construction required for the figure of a panther. A cardboard foundation is covered with low relief sculpture with the pieces bowed out to give a roundness to the animal. In this model the overlays had a cut-out pattern to show the markings which were created by using a black cardboard foundation.

Horses could be constructed on this principle and trimmed with the finery of the circus horse to make attractive pieces.

A decorative lamb of wood construction on the cross-plane method, covered with paper curls for lambswool.

An ideal spring or Easter decoration, it would also serve to accompany a paper-sculptured "Mary" for a nursery rhyme window.

A Wise Old Owl

To make this studious-looking bird, cut out the pattern in cardboard (Fig. 1) and paint black.

The body (Fig. 2) is white paper, and on this will be seen "V" marks in black. Cut each "V" separately with your knife—they are to be raised to show black beneath, thus creating shadows for feather effect.

Attach the bodywork to the foundation by tabs, bowing out the paper in the process. The wings (Fig. 3) are black paper. Cut with the knife where shown, and attach to the back of the body by tabs.

The head (Fig. 4) is also in black paper. Score as indicated, and attach to the foundation by the scored piece and tabs.

The eyes (Fig. 5) are cut to pattern, scored round the dotted lines, and made up by bringing the points to centre. Fasten by sticking patterns cut from black paper—one in each eye—and attach to headpiece (Fig. 6). Score and fold the beak; attach to head.

Cover a tube with wood-design paper—failing paper, a natural twig would serve—curl the claws and fix to twig, fastening the bird behind.

Thus is the bird completed.

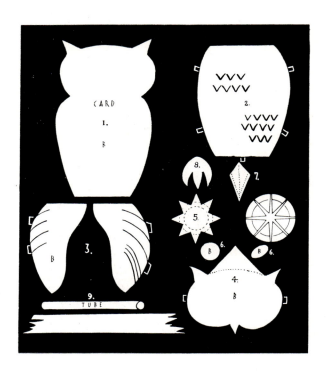

By the author

Here is an idea for a "Wise Buying" feature, for Hallow-e'en decoration, or as a centre piece to an optician's display. The employment of dramatic lighting effects would further enhance the prominence of the model.

Figured in Paper

Evening scene in the park at the Bijenkorf store, Amsterdam

Carol Singers, by the author

Sculptured Figures

Small and simple pieces of full-round sculpture may be no more than tubes or cones—standing by themselves—with a few details added to give them identity. Alternatively, they may be faithful reproductions in miniature.

Students with little sculptural knowledge can take refuge in humorous or naive simplification. A child's or primitive cartoonist's drawing is often very spirited; so, too, can be paper sculpture. But a sufficient background makes for even more telling effects in humour or simplification when they are required.

Figures Made from Cones and Tubes

Let us try making full round figures, using cones and tubes.

These figures are to be small—approximately 18 inches high—and the photograph on the opposite page should be followed as we proceed.

Make a tube (Fig. 1) and trim to the shape shown. Next, a cone (Fig. 2) and two larger cones (Figs. 3 and 4).

Assemble the tube and cones for the face as shown (Fig. 5).

The legs are tubes of paper rolled narrower at one end and stuck together with paste (Fig. 6). Cut out a paper foot and attach (Fig. 7).

The arms are made on the same principle as the legs, with the exception that they are cut and joined to give bending action. Fitting tubes together where they join at different angles is rather a tinsmith's art, but it can be accomplished more easily through trial and error in paper than in a material less tractable.

Fig. 8 shows a straight arm, and Fig. 9 how to cut the tube to join and impart a bent action.

Having cut the tube, place the lower piece over the upper, pushing it over point first. Do not fasten this joint—thus it can be moved. Fig. 10 shows the jointed arm with a cut-out hand added. Fasten the arms and legs to the body.

Fig. 11 shows the finished model with hair added—instructions for making the hair and face features are given on following pages.

As will be seen from the construction of this model, if a figure was required wearing a long skirt or crinoline, the legs would not be needed. All that would be necessary would be a longer cone for the base so that the figure would stand alone.

One method of making the model illustrated stand on its own, is to place a piece of strong wire up one leg and bend the rest into a circle to take the weight of the figure. Alternatively, the figures can be suspended on cotton like puppets.

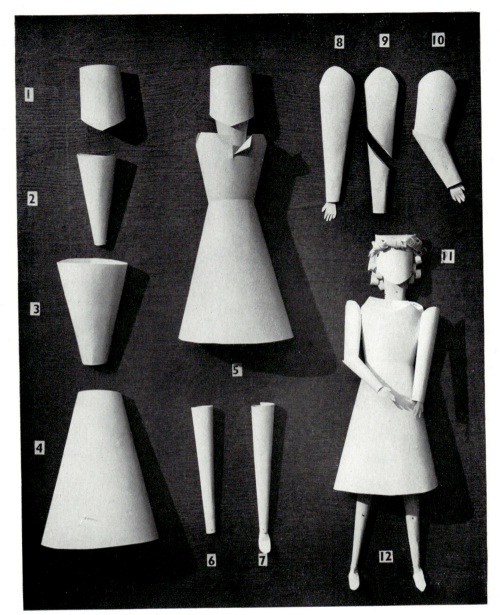

By the author

Features for Sculptured Faces

Cut out a paper face as shown in the drawing on the facing page, and sketch in the features with a pencil.

Cut round the black outline of the ears with a knife, and score the dotted line so that they will bend forward from the face.

From a separate piece of paper, cut out the eyes, nose, and mouth; score down the dotted line and fold.

Fixed to the face with paste, the eyes and mouth are stuck by the top half only so that they stand out in relief and cast a shadow where creased. To complete the figure, stick on the nose and eyebrows.

Details of the finished face can be seen in the photograph below the drawing on the facing page. (A more advanced method of making a face with a sculptured forehead is described on page 50.)

Hair Styles in Paper

In the photograph on the opposite page can be seen a face before the hair is added.

To make the hair style shown (1) cut a piece of paper to pattern, wide at the ends and narrow in the middle.

Try the pattern on the head to test the fit; it may be necessary to experiment with the fitting to obtain perfection. Having cut a suitable pattern, slash each end with scissors.

To curl the hair, take the slashed ends and place them over the scissor blade with your thumb on top, holding the other end firmly in the left hand. Draw your thumb and scissor blade down the paper, and the curl will be effected (see page 18).

On large heads and where there are a number of curls, it may be necessary to curl each separately. For very small hair styles, paper slashed or in ribbon form may be curled by rolling round a pencil.

Having curled the hair, place it in position over the head. Note in hair style (1) that the curls fall over the front of the head and in the opposite direction to curl up at the back.

Style (2) requires a different pattern and less curl.

Style (3) shows how curled pieces are placed one over the other for top curls. Side pieces are cut as pattern, bowed out, and pasted on the side of the head.

Hair styles are very important, especially when making a figure in period costume— see that you have the correct style for the period.

With fashion figures, too, study latest styles of hairdressing as well as clothing.

Cut-out paper face with sketched-in features, and cut-out eyes, nose and mouth marked for folding.

(*Below*) The cut-out face before the hair is added, with methods for three alternative hair styles.

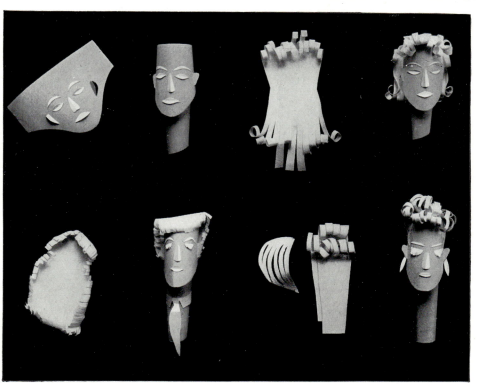

Male Figures

Male figures are constructed upon the same principle as female figures. One large tube comprises the body, a smaller tube the neck, with a tube cut to shape for the face. Two narrow tubes creased and fastened together form the trousers. Arms are tubes cut and joined to give action. Hands, nose, eyes, mouth, etc., are cut flat, then creased in relief and glued to the figure, bent to give dimensional effect.

The headpiece of the male figure should be cut longer than for female figures; the extra length is then cut into strips and turned back over the head to form the hair.

Dressing the Figures

Watch carefully that whichever fashion is selected for your models—modern or period—the style and hair details are correct.

For dressing female figures, the main planes of the dresses are placed one over the other, and the trimmings, pockets, and any other details, are added afterwards.

It is extremely fascinating to study costume design. Making figures and dressing them in historical or national costumes would certainly make history or geography lessons in school far more interesting.

Figures inspired by the ballet *Les Patineurs*, by the author.

"A Chinaman," by the author, made on the cone-and-tube principle.

Superb full-round sculptured figures in a colourful series of pantomime and circus characters which enlivened Dolcis windows in London. Designed and produced by Design & Display, Ltd., London.

(*Top*) Classical costumes by Erica Gorecka-Egan for the exhibition "Costume Carnival." Figures shown are South American poncho, Japanese kimono and Roman draped gown.

(*Below*) Costumes for the ballet by Erica Gorecka-Egan at an exhibition at the New York Museum of Modern Art, illustrating the historic sources to which the costume designer refers for his own imaginative interpretations. Left to right: Costume by Alexandra Vesnin for Racine's *Phedre*; Picasso's design for Satie's *Parade*; and Alexandra Exter's for Oscar Wilde's *Salome*.

Sketch Interpretation

The experienced artist, once he understands the principles and construction of paper sculpture, will be able to sketch his own designs and translate them into the finished work. Interesting subjects for interpretation may also be found in posters, photographs and drawings designed by others. Work which is composed of simple masses with sharp outlines is the best material from which to choose. If one compares paper sculpture with a flat picture the sharp edges take the place of the lines of the composition and the soft ones give it body by the play of light and shade.

On the opposite page is a line and wash drawing of two figures. Let us see how each figure would be translated into low relief paper sculpture. The first step is to analyse how the subject can be divided for pieces of paper sculpture and where the folds and bends could be placed. An overlay of lines on the drawing will indicate these divisions. The next step is to enlarge the drawing to the size required for an experimental model. This can be done either by the photographic method or by the squared system of enlarging. If the latter method is employed draw squares on the drawing. Having decided upon the size of the enlargement draw the same number of squares in proportionate size on to a sheet of drawing paper. Copy the pattern in each small square on the original on to the larger squares, reproducing each line or detail in the same relative position. Enlarging by this method is quite simple and the squares ensure that the correct proportions are adhered to.

Working on the enlarged drawing take a sheet of tracing paper and trace the furthest plane. This would encompass the outline of the figure. This tracing also serves as a pattern for the board foundation of the finished model. The planes in mid-distance are next to be traced on a second sheet of paper and the foreground planes on a third sheet of paper. If the model is to be in colour indicate the colourings on the tracings. Paper patterns are now cut for each piece of a different plane or colour allowing for extra breadth of those pieces that are to bend or fold.

Score and fold the patterns and assemble together temporarily, adjusting them to fit correctly on to a cardboard foundation cut to the outline of the first tracing. The whole is then taken to pieces—marking the pieces for identification—and traced on to the paper to be used for the final work. They can then be cut out and assembled easily for the finished model.

A line and wash drawing to be interpreted into paper sculpture

The drawing with an overlay of outlines to analyse how it can be divided for pieces of paper sculpture

The completed study portrayed in paper sculpture. (See also page 7)

"Dresden Courtier," by the author

This figure was larger-than-life size and made from paper in the colourings of Dresden china.

A figure in brown, scarlet and white paper sculpture larger-than-life size.

"Federal Fashions" at B. Altmans, New York,
featuring an exquisite centre-piece of Washing-
ton in low-relief sculpture in colour. (*Courtesy:
Staples-Smith Studio, New York*)

Paper Sculpture in the Display Window

Scope for the use of paper sculpture in the display window is unlimited. Glancing through this book ideas for using many of the pieces illustrated in conjunction with merchandise are at once suggested.

Paper sculpture has a freshness of appeal combined with distinctive art qualities. It costs considerably less than any other type of decoration and the variation of design is dependent only upon the ingenuity of the creator.

Display decorations are required for short duration. Paper sculpture, after use, presents no problems in its disposal. The fact is that it is light to handle and can be fixed in any desired position. This adds to its popularity for display purposes.

The art of the displayman is often to dramatise merchandise by the use of objects which are not merchandise but which tell a sales story relating to the merchandise or enhancing its saleability by the atmosphere created by such decor. In display the decorations may attract attention but should never overpower the merchandise displayed. Paper Sculpture is ideal in this respect.

Complete display settings can be made in paper sculpture columns, arches, architectural details, baroque frames, etc. Larger-than-life size figures can be made and, being stylised and in a different convention from that of window mannequins, are not incongruous when placed beside them.

At the other extreme miniature figures have a tremendous fascination. They can be used to tell the fashion story of merchandise as, for example, a garden party scene or a wedding group—telling in a small space the sales story of the merchandise displayed. It is useful also to carry out a display theme to feature a department or service—fur storage for example. In this case a most amusing theme could be visualised showing the defeat of moths. Paper sculpture is ideal for such a purpose. A window display of miniature mannequins would be certain to publicise a forthcoming fashion parade.

Anniversary events also call for tableaux showing figures and scenes of the period in which the store was founded, or a birthday cake could be featured with the icing simulated by paper sculpture curlycues complete with candles and surmounted by a figure in costume of the period.

Decorations are used at Christmas time more than at any other and almost all the atmosphere required can be created in paper sculpture, from the complete tableaux telling the whole Christmas story, down to the humble holly leaf required for the corner of a package or showcard.

At Christmas, window displays are often given over to pictorial studies without merchandise, for instance a scene of carol singers or a biblical theme. In this type of display, paper sculpture is at its best, since there is nothing to emphasise its paper construction and it appears as sculpture. Left white and properly lit or with the paper coloured, it makes a most attractive scheme. Lighting enhances the value of paper sculpture by bringing into play the differences of light and shade in the various planes.

Holiday shows in summer suggest seagulls, palm trees, etc. In fact there is not a season that cannot be portrayed or given atmosphere by the use of paper sculpture.

Another great feature of this medium is its use in the showcase within the store. The low relief suggests volume, yet the creation remains flat enough for the shallow showcase and allows for merchandise to be shown.

From this can be seen the possibilities of paper sculpture in the field of visual presentation. This new art form gives life, atmosphere and selling power to the display window.

Inspired by the ballet *Cinderella*, this unique window display features the coach in the background with plume decoration and huge sculptured wings suggesting fantasy. Cinderella shows her beautiful ball dress, and emphasis is placed upon a cinderella shoe in the foreground. This display, which appeared at Jay Thorpe, New York, shows how effective paper sculpture can be for large-scale schemes. (*Courtesy: Marquardt & Co. Inc., New York*)

An original display at B. Altman's, New York. Dressmaker in paper sculpture adds an amusing touch, at the same time explaining the showcard wording "Master-Made Patterns." (*Courtesy: Staples-Smith Studio, New York*)

Clever household linen window at W. J. Sloane, New York. Note paper-sculptured maid and mistress, and the two-colour decoration on the linen cupboard. (*Courtesy: Staples-Smith Studio, New York*)

A further window in the series "Federal Fashions." Centre figure features "Lafayette"; note the details included by the sculptor and the decorative bases upon which they are mounted. (*Courtesy: Staples-Smith Studio, New York*)

Portraying an African witch doctor, this paper sculpture figure was complete with face mask, grass skirt, horns, head-dress, etc. The tie-in with the merchandise was explained on the card, which read "Like a Spell of Old Black Magic." Strong shadows created by lighting on the background added to the air of mystery at Mandel Bros., New York. (*Courtesy: Staples-Smith Studio, New York*)

"Spring breaks through" was apt slogan for a series at Austin Reed. Dapper sparrow in coloured sculptured paper was by Z. Kowalewski. (*Courtesy: Austin Reed*)

Making a Palm Tree

Palm trees for summer displays are often required by a store, and can be made simply and effectively in Paper Sculpture.

For the trunk of the tree, use can be made of a cardboard tube from a roll of linoleum, or similar tube of sufficient strength to form a foundation.

Bore holes in the top of the tube, and wrap the tube with strips of paper approximately 8 inches wide and slashed at intervals as shown in the sketch. Wrap spiral-fashion from top to bottom.

Cut leaves as instructed, and score and crease. Bend where shown on the dotted line; spread a little glue along the bend, and place over a piece of stiff wire.

When the leaves have been completed and are dry, fasten to the tree trunk by inserting them in the holes prepared at the top, and secure.

Palm trees look especially cool when left white against a blue background, or they can be coloured by using a spray gun or employing coloured papers in making.

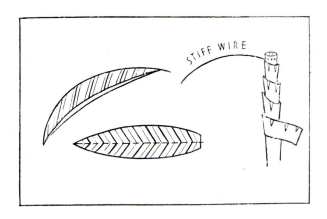

STIFF WIRE

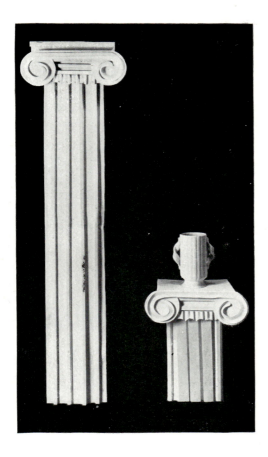

Columns of the type shown on left are a very useful decoration for window display. They must, of course, be built round a foundation if required to stand alone. By the author.

A useful spring decoration is this dovecot; in coloured papers it would be particularly effective. (*Courtesy: Display World, Cincinnati*)

A paper-sculptured palm tree by the author assists in adding atmosphere to this display featuring "Palm Beach" hats.

The large sculptured head of Santa Claus by the author makes an interesting setting for this display of Christmas gifts for men.

A paper-sculptured wildfowl is designed and used here by the author as an attraction in a display of Christy's "Wildfowl" hats.

Paper figures in a Christy hat display by the author.

87

Certain eye-catcher for a display of washing fabrics would be this amusing washerwoman, seen at Abraham Straus', New York. (*Courtesy: Staples-Smith Studio, New York*)

Modern merchandise contrasting with fashions and customs of the 1900's was featured in paper-sculptured panels on the backgrounds. (*Courtesy: Display World, New York*)

Paper sculpture panel showing musical instruments, notes, treble cleff, etc., adding atmosphere to a showing of evening wear at Gimbel's, New York. (*Courtesy: Marquardt & Co. Inc., New York*)

In the centre panel of this display can be seen a sculptured figure of a man. Atmosphere is given by placing it before a painted background. (*Courtesy: Display World, New York*)

This cute hurdy-gurdy man, with his organ and monkey,
would be a certain attraction in a juvenile display. Note
painted backcloth as setting for the figure in this window at
B. Altman & Co., New York. (*Courtesy: Staples-Smith Studio,
New York*)

Sophisticated angel in paper sculpture dominates this gift show at Jay Thorpe, New York. Note novel build-up of the display—on parcels—suggesting the goods as gifts.

A sculptured alligator could not help but draw attention to a display of alligator shoes and handbags. (*Courtesy: Display World, Cincinnati*)

These amusing farmyard friends are from America. Disney-like in character, they would be ideal Easter display pieces if placed in a suitable setting.

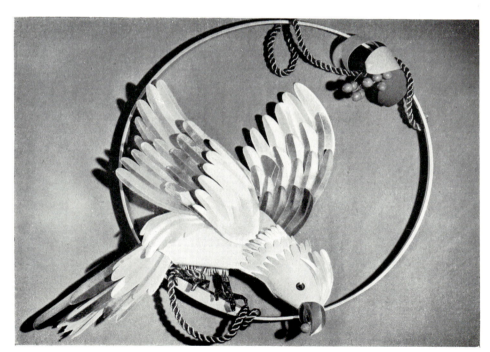

Delightful for a home decoration, this parrot would look its best in vividly coloured papers.

PHOTOGRAPH BY COURTESY OF MARQUARDT & CO. INC., NEW YORK

A delightful study in full colour sculpture. Note the humour in the antics of the frogs; this would make a good spring window display attraction.

The stork on its own would be useful for a baby linen display, and the panel would look amusing as a decoration in a children's wear department.

94

This clever piece of full colour sculpture would be an ideal focusing point in a store interior or window display. Note the use of wood-veneer papers in the construction of the trees and house.

Fireplace of paper sculpture in children's
book window. (*Courtesy: Staples-Smith Studio,
New York*)

Delightful setting for luxury gifts at Berg-dorf Goodmans, New York. Note giant Christmas angel, doves, trees, etc. Paper sculpture in this window was by Erica Gorecka-Egan.

Anniversary Displays

The use of paper sculpture decor for special events is shown in these scenes of fifty years ago. Made for the centenary celebrations of Stix Baer and Fuller, St. Louis, by Ugo Mochi.

They featured nostalgic glimpses of the gay 'nineties designed with period accuracy as well as gaiety and verve. Ugo Mochi is regarded as the world's greatest silhouettist.

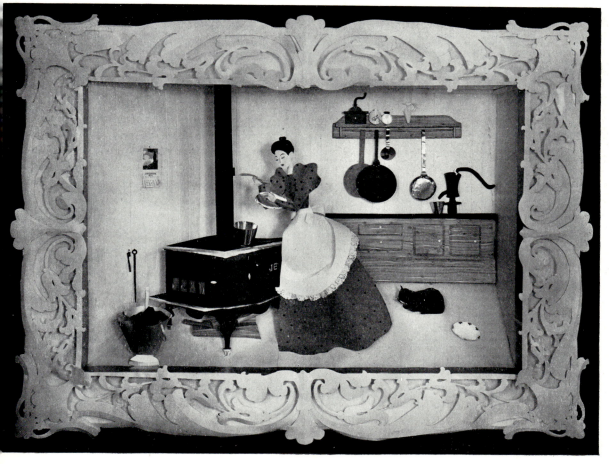

Decor for a Fashion Parade

The figure of a shepherdess shown here was a feature of the decor used for a parade of junior fashions. Larger-than-life size it at once set a new standard in this form of decoration. It was also used in photographic form to decorate the programme cover.

"Shepherdess," by the author

Cut Surface Designs

On the opposite page is an illustration of a playing card. This was made in paper sculpture and it will be noted that much of the work is composed of cutting the surface and raising the paper to create novel effects of light and shade, and also to expose an undersheet of paper of another colour to create contrast. This is a useful technique for feathers on birds (see illustration of the owl on page 61) and the panther below.

Giant playing card using a cut-surface technique, by the author.

Paper Sculpture into Metal Sculpture

Paper Sculpture is a popular medium for interior displays. A new development is its translation into sheet metal for outdoor treatment

Selfridge's famous store is always one of the sights of London on festive occasions. Christmas decorations illustrated took the form of giant nursery rhyme characters developed from paper sculptured cartoons. Each of the figures was animated and appeared in a nursery rhyme book setting, floodlit by huge lamp units camouflaged as balloons.

One of the 2-foot models used as patterns for making the 12-foot figures.

The models were originally made in paper sculpture, 10 inches high. After this they were enlarged to 2 feet high, at which stage they were animated so that details of the movement could be developed by the use of fractional horse-power motors.

From the 2 feet models, paper patterns were then made enlarging the models to 12 feet high, the finished size of those on the building. These patterns were used as templates to guide the metal workers in reproducing the figures exactly in sheet metal. The scheme was a joint operation by a team comprising outside designers and contractors and the store's own display department.

Superb caricature of a huntsman and hounds, by Bruce Angrave, M.S.I.A.

This delightful figure of a faun is by Erica Gorecka-Egan, New York.

Theatre
Publicity

"Cousin Cora," a character from the play *Life with Father*. By Erica Gorecka-Egan, New York.

"Mary Skinner,"
another character from
the play *Life with Father*.
These figures were used
to publicise the play in
New York. Designed by
Erica Gorecka-Egan,
New York.

Publicity

A figure to publicise a fashion parade. Made
in metallic and plain paper by the author.

Christmas Greetings
to
LONDON
from the
Staff and Management
of
LONDON TRANSPORT

A poster using
a paper
sculpture by
Bruce Angrave,
M.S.I.A.

*(Courtesy:
London Transport)*

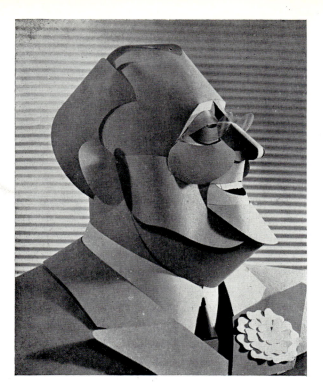

Paper
Cartoons

Cartoons of the late President Roosevelt and Marshal Stalin. By Bruce Angrave, M.S.I.A., famous designer and illustrator.

These examples show a technique of interlocking and splicing paper, thus eliminating the use of adhesives

Cartoons in paper by Bruce Angrave, designed for the *Modern Woman* stand at the Ideal Home Exhibition Deft handling, concise lines and humorous characterisation are Angrave's distinctive trade marks.

Book
Covers

These three illustrations emphasise how skill can be brought to bear in designing humorous figures by naive simplification.

The work of Mall Sinclair, an artist working in Canada, they were designed for the covers of *Menswear Merchandising*, by whose kind permission they are reproduced.

Paper sculpture reproduces well for book covers and illustrations if adequately lighted for photographing.

The effect of the figures is greatly enhanced by the tiny settings and by the superb lighting and photography.

Paper Sculpture for Exhibitions

By Tadeusz Lipski

The idea of creating atmosphere in miniature is often required for exhibition purposes, since space is often limited, or, as was the case with the Royal Arms panel above, it can be used on a gigantic scale to attract the eye.

Some very fine examples of paper sculpture were seen at the *Daily Herald* "Post-war Homes" exhibition, staged at Dorland Hall.

Pictured at top right is the panel which introduced the exhibition to visitors — the *Daily Herald* cockerel.

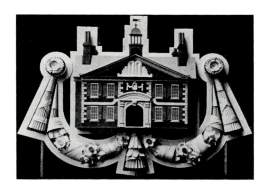

Paper sculpture was used with cardboard architectural models in relief, by Tadeusz Lipski.

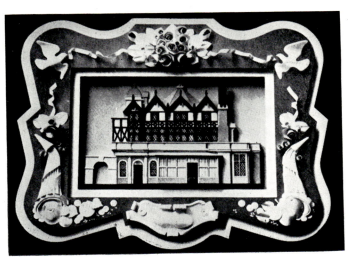

Advertising Layout

Paper-sculptured birds with paper ribbons. An advertising layout for a children's wear manufacturers, giving an unusual and dainty effect. By the author, for H. & E. Hughsley Ltd., London.

A Painting of Paper Sculpture

"The Water is Wide," by Marion Adnams (1940)

Here is a study by Marion Adnams which employs a paper-sculptured figure in the composition. The superb colouring of the painting is part of its charm and cannot, of course, be seen in this black-and-white reproduction.

Note the artist's skill in making the figures, which is, however, only a means to an end; the end being the delightful manner in which she paints them, imparting an atmosphere of fantastic beauty.

The figures could not be mistaken for anything but paper; the technique in painting them faithfully reproduces the lightness of a paper construction.

Many of Miss Adnams' paintings are in private collections, and two are exhibited at the Manchester City Art Gallery. (*Courtesy: Mrs. Malcolm Hayes*)

Crossed Plane Construction

Crossed-plane technique, although it is more familiar with the making of toys and cardboard ornaments, can be applied to paper sculpture.

Solid volume may be suggested not only by a shell over a framework but by the framework itself. The uprights and roofs beams of a frame house, before the walls and roof are covered in, give a convincing image of a house. Thus, a couple of crossed squares, as sketched here, suggest the volume of a solid cube. The animals shown in the sketch also interpret this technique and, while convincing in themselves, could be covered with curled paper, thus giving a full solid effect.

 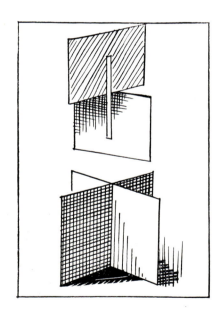

On the opposite page, this crossed-plane technique can be seen applied to the construction of the stoppers on the decanters [lower illustration], and the framework construction—suggesting volume—in the decanters themselves. Note that the principle of construction is closely allied to the manner in which Christmas lanterns are made in kindergarten.

Tadeusz Lipski, the Polish artist, was responsible for this superb
creation made to publicise the Cocktail Bar at Lyon's Corner House,
London.

The sculpture was white against a sky-blue background, and the
bottles and grapes were plaster.

"Jovial Santa Claus," by the author

This portrayal of Santa Claus was executed in full-round paper sculpture in red, black and white, 5 feet in height. Ideal for a "Toy Fair" in a store or at a Christmas party, it would also be a welcome gift for the children's ward of a local hospital.

126

Metallics for paper sculpture can produce some very effective results, as can be seen in this figure of an angel. Decorations in this material must be styled with very little scoring, since the under-paper will show through the scored surface.

Courtesy:
Staples-Smith Studio,
New York

These delightful and amusing cherubs in a holly wreath were executed in
full colour sculpture, and would be a great attraction in a window display or
for a column decoration.

Courtesy: Marquardt & Co. Inc., New York

This gay and humorous elephant would assure attention to a display and find popularity with the children at a toy fair. Entirely different for a Christmas tree decoration, it could also be used in a circus atmosphere.

Courtesy: Marquardt & Co. Inc., New York

Nativity Panel
Decoration

By the author

From the exercise in making a fan, you will see at a glance how easily this decorative panel is constructed.

Made in an all-white paper on a scarlet background, it would also be highly attractive in metallic papers, and would form pleasing Christmas decoration.

A circle of cardboard for the centre is required, which should be large enough to accommodate the moulding round the panel and the silhouette figures.

Cut out the figures and mount them on the circle; these are purposely left flat for reasons of simplicity. The star is the only part actually sculptured, and one of these was made in the exercise on page 21.

Cut a circle of paper for the moulding, which should be approximately 3 inches larger than the actual size of panel. This is scored (dotted line in sketch) and cut as shown. Crease where scored, at the same time moulding into a circle, and fit to the frame. By this, you will see that it requires overlapping where cut, to enable it to fit. When assembled together, apply paste to the joins and place on one side to set and secure.

The outer frame is made on the same principle as in making a fan, excepting that it is cut to the shape shown in the sketch. Cut sufficient of these shapes to fit round the entire centre panel, score and fold them, and fit to the back of the centre panel fan-fashion the whole way round. Fastening can be effected by either pins or gummed tape.

Turn the panel over to the front again, and complete by fixing the moulding made for the centre; the frame is considerably improved if mounted on a panel carrying the same colour as the centre.

This attractive Christmas panel is noteworthy for its simplicity in making. Pleating forms the border, fir leaves, and rays of the candle. The candle is simply a tube, with a flame of paper. This panel was executed by the author in white paper, with a green border to the centre panel.

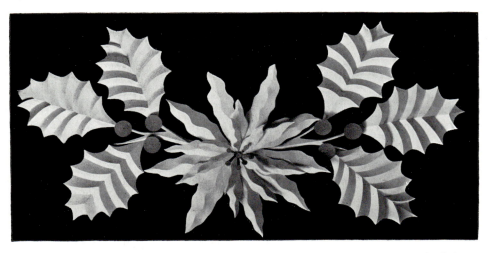

Here is a decoration made by the author on the scoring and folding principle in scarlet and white, on a green background.

The Star and Wreath design by the author shown on left employs the holly leaf and star, finished with a sculptured bow.

Holly Leaf Decoration

Draw a holly leaf on a piece of drawing paper as shown in the illustration. Mark the veins on both sides of the paper with a pencil, using dotted and plain lines.

On one side of the leaf score the strong lines only, and on the reverse side the dotted lines. With both hands, mould the heavy lines down and the dotted lines up. This is a little more difficult than folding a fan, because the lines are not straight.

The berry is a circle of paper cut to the centre as shown. "A" is pulled round to "B" and stuck with paste.

Christmas Tree Decoration

By the author

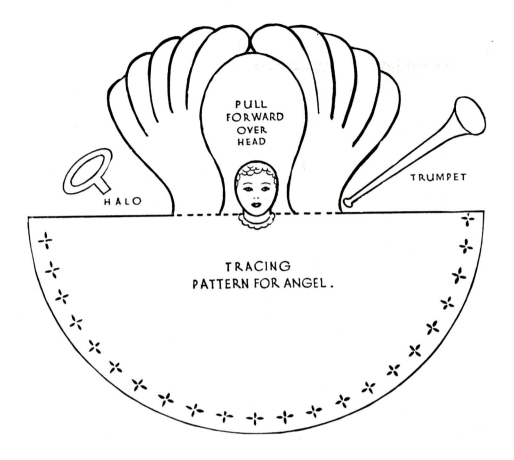

PULL
FORWARD
OVER
HEAD

HALO

TRUMPET

TRACING
PATTERN FOR ANGEL.

To make the angel, draw the pattern and cut out, taking great care round the head. Pull the piece of paper where marked over the head. Roll the end of this piece round a pencil—this will make a scroll.

Now bend the figure into a cone and fasten at the back with Seccotine. Bend the wings slightly forward. The halo is cut out and fixed behind the head. The trumpet is fixed to the body behind the scroll.

These figures look delightful for Xmas tree or table decoration.

Starting a Studio

Here are a few hints for the sculptor who wishes to start a studio. Since paper sculpture relies on the play of light and shade upon its planes for effect, the first essential of the studio is good lighting—both artificial and daylight. Ample table surface will be required and, the table tops where cutting is to be carried out, should be protected with cardboard as well as sheets of paper, which can be removed when they become slashed and uneven.

A stock of paper in white and colours should be kept as the right sheet for a particular job is always evasive when urgently required. The sheets of paper should be kept flat and deep shelves provided in which to store them. Drawers and cupboards will be needed to house tools, etc. Staples, nails, tacks, wire, adhesives and other oddments used in the construction of paper sculpture should not be forgotten and the tidy mind will ensure that they are always in the same place—ready for use when required. Cardboard, wallboard and other stout foundation materials are also needed. A bandsaw or Cutawl machine will be necessary for cutting the board foundations for the larger pieces of sculpture. A strong staple gun of the type used by displaymen will be needed in order to fasten the paper sculptures to hard foundations. Bins will be needed to hold scraps of paper in order to keep the studio tidy and avoid the danger of fire from the collection of such waste material.

While pieces of sculpture are in the making they should be covered with dust sheets at night or the work will collect dust when the studio is swept.

When construcing large pieces of sculpture note that size of the studio door and see that there is ample space to permit removal of the work. If the door is too small to allow free passage the construction will have to be made in sections. In this connection an important item to bear in mind when considering a commission is the ultimate site for the work and its accessibility.

Installation

White paper sculpture should be kept scrupulously clean and all pencil marks, finger marks, etc., removed before installation. If these details are not observed all illusion of being solid is lost.

Paper sculpture must be handled with care whilst being installed since crushing, dropping or tearing will necessitate repairs. Small tears can be repaired with gum tape affixed to the back of the work, but repairs are never satisfactory and the best rule is to avoid damage by careful handling.

One of the main features of paper sculpture is its extreme lightness. It is also stronger than one at first imagines. It can be moved and fixed in any position with little effort. Low relief pieces can be fixed to window or showcase backs with staples or tacks. Full round pieces can stand alone and be placed where they can be viewed from all sides. They can also be suspended with nylon threads giving the effect of floating in space. It is advisable, when displaying paper sculpture in the department store or at an exhibition, to place it out of reach of curious fingers.

Notes on Packing and Storage

Paper sculpture may have to be dispatched some distance from where it is made. Because of its lightness freight charges are small. It must, however, be securely packed to prevent crushing, preferably in a strong box or crate lined with waterproof paper. Excessive dampness or a spatter of rain will ruin the work. Pack each piece so that no part touches the sides of the container to rub or dent. If possible tack the work to the case by its foundation to prevent movement and use light braces of paper, stapled in place, to hold rigidly the pieces that cannot be fastened by other means. To store sculptured pieces for subsequent re-use, they should be wrapped to keep out dust and, if practicable, should be boxed.

Education

Many schools have added paper sculpture to their curriculum. It has unquestionable educational value as a means of self expression.

The simple demands of this medium in tools and materials make it ideally suitable for the classroom.

Paper Sculpture gives the student the satisfaction of producing something worth while in design and practical application. Having enjoyed an enviable popularity in Advertising and Window Display for some years, its continued popularity in many spheres opens up an exciting new field for the art student planning a career in Display, Design and Decoration.

If my efforts in compiling this book prove useful in some of the directions mentioned, it will have been well worth while.

By Mall Sinclair

ACKNOWLEDGMENTS

The development of paper sculpture has resulted from the activities of many artists—both here and abroad—some of whom have afforded material for this book.

Grateful thanks are offered to all those who have helped by providing specimens of their work, and particularly to:

Marquardt & Co. Inc., New York, for photographs and data concerning applications of the craft in America.

Mr. William A. Vickers for the finished drawings and sketches illustrating the instructional pages.

Tunbridge Studio and Campbell's Press Studio, for collaboration and interest in the photography of my work.

Mr. Leslie W. Goss for his assistance and friendly interest in the preparation of the book.

I also wish to thank all those anonymous artists in paper sculpture whose work appears in the window displays shown herein, where it has been possible to acknowledge only the stores concerned.
A.S.

144